The Story of
SHABBAT

by Molly Cone

illustrated by Emily Lisker

HarperCollins*Publishers*

For Nathan, Hannah, Sarah, and Samuel
—M.C.

To Gabriel and Rose
—E.L.

The illustrations in this book were painted in acrylic on canvas.

The text for this book was first published in *The Jewish Sabbath,* a Crowell Holiday Book edited by Susan Bartlett Weber, written by Molly Cone, and illustrated by Ellen Raskin in 1966.

The Story of Shabbat
Text copyright © 1966, 2000 by Molly Cone
Illustrations copyright © 2000 by Emily Lisker
Printed in the U.S.A. All rights reserved.
http://www.harperchildrens.com

Library of Congress Cataloging-in-Publication Data
Cone, Molly.   The story of Shabbat / by Molly Cone;
illustrated by Emily Lisker.   p.   cm.   Text for this
book was first published in The Jewish Sabbath. New York :
Crowell, 1966.   Summary: Explains the history and traditions that
are part of the Jewish holiday of Shabbat.   ISBN 0-06-027944-3. —
ISBN 0-06-027945-1 (lib. bdg.)   1. Sabbath—Juvenile literature.
[1. Sabbath.]   I. Lisker, Emily, ill.   II. Cone, Molly.   Jewish Sabbath.   III. Title.
BM685.C66   2000   98-16626   296.4′1—dc21   CIP   AC
Typography by Elynn Cohen

1   2   3   4   5   6
7   8   9   10
❖
First
Edition

The Story of
SHABBAT

Candlelighting means *Sabbath* to many Jewish children, for they know the Sabbath in a Jewish home begins with candlelighting. With candlelighting and blessing. First the candlelighting, then the blessing, and after that there are good things to eat in honor of the Sabbath.

The Sabbath is a special day to the Jewish people. From the moment it begins just before sunset on Friday evening to the moment it ends after sunset on Saturday evening, it has a special feeling.

Perhaps this is because the Sabbath is different from all the other days of the week. It is a holiday. It is the Day of Rest.

The idea of the Sabbath goes back to the beginning of the world as the Hebrew Bible tells it. God created the world in six days, and on the seventh day God rested. The seventh day was called the Sabbath. The word *Sabbath* comes from a Hebrew word, *Shabbat*. It means *rest*.

Sunday is the Sabbath for most Christians. And Friday is the Sabbath for Muslims. But Saturday has always been the Sabbath to Jews. It is the oldest holiday they celebrate.

The keeping of the Sabbath is a law to the Jewish people. It is an important part of their Torah. *Torah* is what they call the learning they live by. On the Jewish Sabbath it is against the law to mourn. And against the law to worry. And against the law to work.

And how this law came to be is the story of the Sabbath.

A long, long time ago a people speaking Hebrew came to live in the land of Egypt. They came with great joy, for one of their tribesmen, Joseph, was already there. He was honored by the Egyptian pharaoh, or king, so Joseph's people, the Jews, lived there happily for many years.

Another pharaoh rose to rule in Egypt. He did not like the strangers in his land. He set tasks for them. And the harder they worked, the more work he gave them to do.

A lake cannot give water and never be refilled. A field cannot grow grain and never lie fallow. A person cannot work and never be refreshed. The lake becomes a dry bed. The field, barren ground. And the person— a slave.

The Jews became slaves in Egypt.

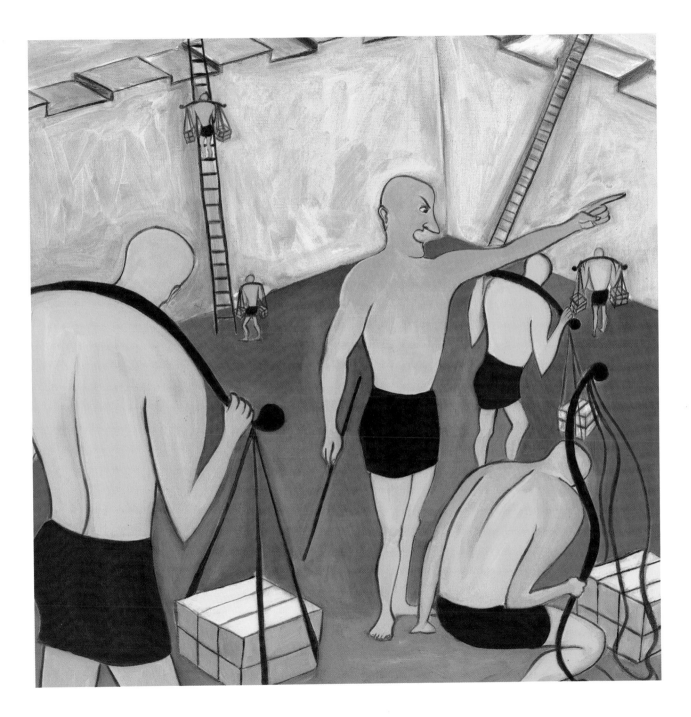

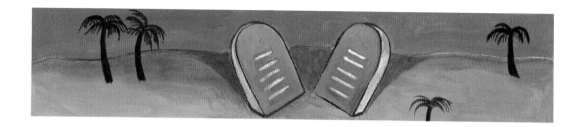

With God's help Moses led the Jews out of the land of Egypt. The Bible tells how God looked after them. It tells how God gave them the Ten Commandments as the law for free people to live by.

And in the Fourth Commandment the Jews found the way to make freedom a part of their lives forever.

The Fourth Commandment says:

"Remember the Sabbath day and keep it holy. Six days you shall labor and do all your work, but the seventh day is the Sabbath. On it you shall do no manner of work; not you, nor your son, nor your daughter, nor your servants, nor the animals in your house, nor the stranger within your gates. For in six days God made heaven and earth and sea, and all that is in them, and God rested on the seventh day. . . ."

When the Jewish people left Egypt and settled in the land of Israel, they made this Fourth Commandment their way of life. Like God, they did their work in six days. Like God, they rested on the seventh. And they gave the animals who worked in their fields this time for rest, too.

The blowing of a *shofar* reminded everyone to stop work for the Sabbath. As the daylight faded to darkness, two candles were lit to mark the beginning of the Sabbath. From sundown on Friday to after sundown on Saturday, no work was done. No gathering of wood, no lighting of fires, no cooking. Work was against the law on the Sabbath.

As the centuries passed, the Jewish people spread out to other parts of the world. But they kept the Sabbath no matter where they were. In Europe many hundreds of years ago, poor Jews ate only dark bread all week long. But on the Sabbath rich and poor alike ate white bread. To honor the day, the bread dough was braided before it was baked. Sabbath candles and the Sabbath loaf became symbols of the Day of Rest.

In the little Jewish towns and villages the Sabbath was the day for study. The people gathered together in a *synagogue* to read the Torah. Then men talked about the stories it told and argued about what the stories meant. The Sabbath day of study filled the Jewish people's heads with new thoughts. Thus, their minds as well as their bodies were renewed on the day of rest.

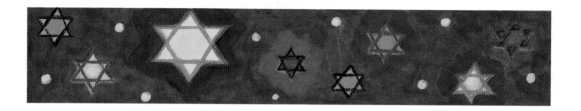

The Sabbath became the very heart of Judaism, the Jewish religion.

History records how Jews held on to their Sabbath even when they were persecuted or exiled. The Sabbath kept their hopes alive. Long ago a poet wrote a poem about the magic of the Jewish Sabbath.

In the poem an evil witch turned a handsome prince into an ugly dog. But the witch's evil spell could not work on the Sabbath. On the Sabbath the ugly dog became a prince again!

The poem was not just a fairy tale, for Jews often felt persecuted in those days. Only on the Sabbath did those Jews feel like themselves again.

There are many stories about the special feeling of the Sabbath. One tells about a rich Persian who loved all manner of good things.

Passing a Jewish home on a Friday night, he smelled a delicious smell. He asked what was cooking on the stove, and took the recipe home to his wife.

But the delicious smell he had expected did not come from the soup his wife made from the recipe. The Persian wondered what was missing. So the next Friday afternoon he again stopped at the Jewish house and made careful note of everything that went into the pot.

"Bah!" said the Persian, after sniffing into the second kettle of soup his wife made. "This is still not the same!"

"The Jew is playing a trick on you!" the wife said angrily. "There must be a secret seasoning!"

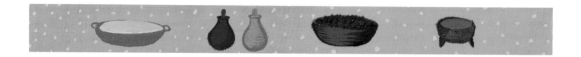

The next Friday the Persian returned to the Jew's house.

"Tell me, what is it that makes everything smell so good in this house every Friday night?" he demanded.

The Jew looked about his small home. The Sabbath candles spread their light over the dinner table. The Sabbath loaves lay ready under their napkin cover. A cup of wine stood by.

As it was every Sabbath at this time, all work had been put away. Food for the next day had been prepared. The room sparkled; the floor was swept clean. His wife and children sat at the table with the glow of the Sabbath on their faces. It was true—a delicious aroma seemed to fill the house.

"You have a secret seasoning!" the Persian said accusingly. "What is it?"

The Jew smiled. "The Sabbath itself is the seasoning that makes everything taste so good," he said.

Today, though many Sabbath customs have changed since ancient times, the Sabbath feeling is still the same.

In many Jewish homes the table is laid with a fine cloth on Friday night. The Sabbath dinner is the best of the week. Just before the sun goes down, the mother or someone else in the family lights the Sabbath candles. Softly, all say the blessing over them.

The father or another family member then holds up the cup of wine, and everyone joins in reciting the special blessing over it. The wine is for the joy of the Sabbath. This is the time parents put their hands on the heads of their children and bless them. Then, all together, they say the blessing over the Sabbath loaf, and each eats a piece from it.

The blessings are recited in Hebrew. They are thank-yous to God. They thank God for the Torah and for the Sabbath, the Day of Rest. They thank God for life and home and family and the good food on the table.

"Good Sabbath!" is what everyone says after the blessings are recited. Or "Shabbat Shalom," which means "Sabbath Peace to You." Then everyone eats the good things made to celebrate the Sabbath.

All over the world, Jewish families begin the celebration of the Sabbath on Friday night. Many go to their synagogues and temples before dinner. Others go after dinner. Some go on Saturday morning or Saturday afternoon. In a Jewish home, on the Sabbath day, the whole house is at rest.

Some people rest by closing their eyes and thinking. Some rest by walking, or visiting friends, or reading, or playing. Resting means being free to just be.

A person thinks a little bigger on the Sabbath. A person stands a little taller on the Sabbath. A person is a *person* on the Sabbath.

When three stars are seen in the sky on Saturday night, the Sabbath day is ended. In many Jewish homes good-bye to the Day of Rest is said with blessings too.

A wine cup is filled until the wine runs over. "May the coming week overflow with goodness like the wine in the cup," the head of the family says. A box of spices is passed around. The good spice smell reminds everyone of the sweetness of the Sabbath just past.

A last farewell is made over a lighted candle. It is a special candle of twisted strands. It is called a Havdalah candle. *Havdalah* means *Separation.* The Havdalah blessings separate the holiday from the weekday.

The leader takes a sip of the wine, then dips the lighted candle into the cup. The flame goes out. The dusk has turned to darkness, and the Sabbath is over. But its goodness is remembered all through the week.

Making Challah Bread

This braided white bread is the traditional Sabbath loaf (pronounce it _hal la_).

What you will need:

measuring cups and spoons
small bowl
large wooden spoon
large bowl
breadboard
clean dish towel
baking sheet
pastry brush

$1/3$ cup lukewarm water. (Stick your finger in it. If the water feels neither hot nor cold, it is just right.)
1 package active dry yeast
2 tablespoons sugar
$1^3/4$ cups flour
$1/2$ teaspoon salt
1 egg, lightly beaten
$1/4$ cup sweet butter or margarine, melted

And:

extra flour to knead the dough
extra butter or margarine to grease the bowl and baking sheet, or a nonstick cooking spray

1 beaten egg for brushing top
1 teaspoon sesame seeds or poppy seeds, if desired, to sprinkle on top

1) Put the lukewarm water into the small bowl. Add the yeast and a pinch of the sugar and mix. Let this mixture sit until bubbly (about 5 to 10 minutes).

2) Place the flour in the large bowl. Stir in the remaining sugar, the salt, and the yeast mixture. Add one egg and the butter or margarine. Mix well.

3) Sprinkle some of the extra flour on a clean breadboard or countertop. Flour your hands and then turn the dough out onto it. Sprinkle a little flour over the dough if it is sticky.

4) Fold the dough in half. Knead it by pushing it down and away with the heel of your hand. Rotate the dough a quarter turn, fold the dough in half again, and push some more. Continue refolding, rotating, and kneading several minutes, until the dough feels like a smooth ball. Add a sprinkle of flour if the dough feels sticky.

5) Place the ball in the bowl greased with the extra butter or margarine. Cover with the dish towel. Let the dough rise for about 1 hour or until it doubles in size.

6) Uncover and punch the dough down with your fist. Turn it out onto the breadboard. Knead it again gently a few times, and divide into 3 equal balls. Let the balls rest for about 15 minutes on the board.

7) Now roll each ball into a rope that's about 16 inches long. Starting in the center, braid the ropes together toward each end. Pinch the ends together.

8) Grease the baking sheet with the extra butter or margarine. Gently lift the challah onto the baking sheet. Cover the challah with the dish towel and let it rise again until it is double in size. This should take about 25 to 35 minutes.

9) Turn on the oven to 350° degrees so it can preheat.

10) With the pastry brush spread the beaten egg over the challah. If you like, sprinkle the top with sesame or poppy seeds.

11) When the oven is ready, bake the challah for 20 to 25 minutes or until golden brown.

Making a Challah Cover

It is customary to cover the challah until the blessing is offered.

What you will need:

1 yellow and 1 blue paper napkin,
    each 12 inches square
4 pieces of red yarn, each about 12
    inches long

scissors
hole puncher

Start with the blue napkin. Fold it in half, then fold it in half again so it makes a square. Cut small shapes and designs from the folded edges of the napkin, the way you would cut a paper snowflake. Open the napkin all the way to see the pretty design you have cut.

Place the cut blue napkin over the open yellow napkin. The yellow color will show through the cuts in the blue napkin.

Line up the edges and corners of the two napkins. Use the hole puncher to make a hole through both napkins at each of the four corners. Gently tie the two napkins together by threading one piece of yarn through each of the double holes. Tie each piece of yarn in a bow.